HOPE TRAUMA GROUP: INDIVIDUAL EXERCISES

George F. Rhoades, Jr., Ph.D.

Shantae Williams, Psy.D.

Ana Lisa Phifer, M.A

©2019

L.L. Maxwell Publications

P.O. Box 1164

Pearl City, HI 96782

This manual is dedicated to all the victims, survivors and overcomers of sexual trafficking!

SESSIONS

Week 1
Becoming Part of the Game

Introduction:

Please share your favorite color and favorite cartoon.

____
____
____

Please give your reaction to the following quote: *"Little girls and boys don't dream of one day growing up and being a prostitute!"* ____
____
____

Rosie's Story:

Rosie has very few memories before age six. She does have a few memories of her Mom loving her when she was very young, but even those memories stopped at age five. Rosie had learned how to not move when she was sleeping at night. Every night she would stay awake as long as she could and listen very carefully for noises outside her bedroom. When she heard the floor creak or the brushing of someone on the entry to her room, she froze. She pretended to be asleep, hoping that the person would believe she was asleep and would not touch her again. She is not sure who is touching her on top and under her clothes, because she keeps her eyes shut. She does recognize the voice, but she is afraid of telling her Mom. She says to herself, "It is my fault", especially when sometimes the touching feels good.

What would you say to Rosie? Why is it not her fault for the molestation or abuse?____
____
____
____

Becoming Part of the Game: When first abused before age 6, a child will often blame themselves for that abuse and all that happens bad to them throughout their lives. What would you share with Rosie about these following scenarios?

Rosie's Mom has a boyfriend who invites his friends over for parties and the friends start touching her just like when she was little. As she becomes older they start to do more and more things to her. She has noticed some of the friends giving money to the mom's boyfriend before they take her into her bedroom. . .

---

and/or . . .

Rosie grows up very angry at her Mom for not protecting her and always choosing her boyfriend over taking care of Rosie. In high school her coach offers her a way of making quick money. She just has to go on "dates" with friends of the coach. She carries an extra phone that often vibrates in the classroom. She asks to go to the bathroom, but instead goes to the parking lot where she has a quick "car date." She returns to her classroom after putting things back into her school locker. . .

---

and/or . . .

Rosie feels like she has never had a family, so she felt good to be invited to be part of a club of sorts with fellow teens. She has started to carry a rag of color and knows what parts of town she can and cannot go to. She gets the drugs she wants and is shared by the group sexually. Sometimes she is asked to do sex for her group with people outside of the group. This is her way of being loyal to the group. . .

---

and/or . . .

Rosie has learned as a teenager to deaden her pain with drugs; she burns almost daily and pops pills whenever they are available. She has tried ice but prefers "bars." Sometimes when she is hungry or needs drugs, she trades sexual favors for the money or drugs. . .

---

and/or . . .

Rosie has very few friends, so when one of the popular girls invited her to a party (without parents) at their house, she went with no hesitation. There was so many teens at the party and a couple of really cool dressed guys. Her friend gave her a class of coke and she started feeling strange. She was led into a bedroom to rest and didn't wake up till hours later. She was naked and knew that someone had sex with her. One of the guys was there with a camera in his hand. The popular girl was next to him. He told her that she had "wild sex" and that he got it all on camera. He said that she had to do what he asked or he would send a copy of the tape to her parents and to everyone at her school. . .

____

____

____

and/or . . .

Rosie has never really had a boyfriend, so when the man started cruising by her in his fancy car she was intrigued. Daily the handsome man would tell her that she was beautiful and asked her if she needed a ride to school. Soon she was given a daily ride to school and received many gifts from the handsome man. They started to have sex and she felt loved. Soon the new boyfriend asked for her help and she started having sex to help her "boyfriend." She left school and her parents and moved in with the boyfriend, surprised that there was several other girls living in the same apartment. . .

____

____

____

Homework: Please write out below how you were brought into "The Game." Please share this with your therapist in individual therapy.

____

____

____

____

____

____

____

____

____

____

____

____

Week 2
Breaking Habits of the Game
(Knowing Who You Are)

Introduction: Share a fun fact about yourself that the group does not know.

____

____

____

What is a habit?

A habit is an acquired behavior pattern regularly followed until it has become almost involuntary.

In "The Game," habits are commonly formed during grooming, seasoning, and turning out. Traffickers/Pimps use isolation, sweet talk, and brainwashing (through music, movies, and videos) to mold your behaviors. Once you're in "The Game" these behaviors become second nature (or habits) and when you leave "The Game" they do not just go away; you have to consciously work to change them, just like your trafficker/pimp put in the time to create the habits, you have to put in the time to break these habits.

What are habits from "The Game" you struggle to break? What would be your reactions/advice be to Rosie in the different scenarios below?

Rosie covers her body at all times and is reluctant to give hugs. She doesn't want anyone to get the wrong idea from her behavior.

____

____

____

and/or. . .

Rosie dresses up wherever she goes and shows a lot of skin. She can't be seen outside of where she lives without full make-up.

____

____

____

and/or. . .

Rosie knows how to look nice on the outside, but she doesn't shower or take care of herself. Sometimes she says to herself, it serves the guys right, because they are dirty "Johns."

____

____

____

and/or. . .

Rosie seems to always be swearing, even when she is not angry. It is just natural to drop the "F" bombs in almost every sentence.

____

____

____

and/or. . .

Rosie has a hard time saving any money, she spends it as fast as she gets it. She gets very upset when she has no money to buy what she wants, i.e. make-up, clothes, shoes, etc. She is thinking that if she has a quick "date" she can get what she wants.

____

____

____

and/or. . .

Rosie has been out of "The Game" for a while and she thinks she can now do "dates" and keep all the money.

____

____

____

What habits from "The Game" have you successfully broken and how did you overcome these habits?

____

____

____

____

This week's assignment: Be mindful of all of your thoughts and actions throughout the week. Specifically focus on the habits from "The Game" you continue to struggle with, when you notice yourself engaging in these thoughts or behaviors, stop yourself and do something different (call someone, journal, whatever is healthy and will help you). Please share what you have discovered and learned in your individual therapy.

____

____

____

Week 3
Breaking Trauma Bonds (Lies and Truth)

Introduction: Please share the most dramatic thing you have done for someone you love(d).

____

____

____

What are Trauma Bonds? Trauma Bonds are defined as an almost unbreakable link between two persons, created and solidified by severe pain or trauma. The Trauma Bond continues past the pain often in an unconscious manner.

Human trafficking in general and in sexual trafficking specifically, these bonds are made to trap the person and to offer them no room to escape. An elephant is a very strong animal, but it can be trained to not attempt escape. A shackle and heavy chain is often used to let the elephant know it can never escape. After much trauma in trying to escape, the elephant does not try to fight against its shackles. The heavy chain now can be exchanged for a rope and the elephant won't try to break free.

A person who is continually beaten learns the consequence of any willful or rebellious actions. The violation of sexual abuse further deepens the trauma bond, often combining love, sexual excitement and violence. To join with the abuser often leads to less trauma and a sense that the trauma is not that bad, or even deserved.

Trauma bonds are also bonds between two or more people that find its root in trauma. The type of trauma experienced does not have to be physical pain, but can also be neglect, betrayal, and emotional abuse. In sex trafficking, this is seen when friends who have trauma histories (i.e. bullying, molestation, non-acceptance, etc.) are introduced into "The Game" by a trafficker/pimp/recruiter/queen mom and begin engaging in sex trafficking together. These friends often feel a kinship because they finally find someone who thinks and feels as they do, making the sex trafficking easier and at times fun. What is not realized is the person who introduced them into "The Game" had ulterior motives and is gaining from their trafficking in some form. In addition, because these friendships are formed from prior unhealed trauma, the friends are not in a space to make positive decisions and end up further traumatizing themselves. Relationships formed from trauma often lead to substance abuse and criminal behaviors, with the end results being severe drug addiction, STD's, pregnancy, incarceration and/or death.

Women are particularly susceptible to bonding to those who traumatize them. Women have their very own mixed blessing in the form of oxytocin. Oxytocin is referred to as the bonding hormone and is the chemical that starts the birth process. It is the reason any woman has a second child, as it prevents memory consolidation. If they were to fully remember the pain of childbirth, it is unlikely they would repeat the experience.

It is believed that trauma in human/sexual trafficking also produce these same trauma bonds that are not easily remembered in the same level of trauma as they actually occurred.

What are your trauma bonds? What insight or advice would you give Rosie in the following scenarios?

Rosie is the youngest in the stable or group of girls living in the house with her pimp. He has beaten her, but also expresses his love for her. She believes that she is his favorite and she loves him.

____

____

____

and/or. . .

Rosie was arrested and refused to share about any other girls and the pimp. She will spend some time in jail and other types of legal confinement. A Social Worker encourages her that she can leave "The Game" but she goes right back to the pimp after being released.

____

____

____

and/or. . .

Rosie's pimp has been arrested and she continues to "work." Rosie saves all the monies that she gets each night and from every date. She will give the monies to the Pimp when he returns.

____

____

____

and/or. . .

Rosie wants to escape, but the pimp has threatened to kill her parents or kidnap her sisters and brothers and "turn them out" on the streets.

____

____

____

and/or. . .

Rosie was taken to the ER due to being beaten by a "John." She now has a chance to leave "The Game" but she can't leave her "sisters" by themselves. She will return to the life once she is discharged from the hospital.

____

____

____

and/or. . .

Rosie was arrested for prostitution and was facing going to jail. She decided to "flip" on her pimp and told law enforcement almost everything about their relationship. She wasn't in love with him, yet she finds herself missing him and regretting getting him into trouble. He always made her promise to never tell on him, and she made that promise over and over. Now Rosie feels guilty.

____

____

____

and/or. . .

Rosie's tired of being in "The Game". She was on the run but decided to turn herself in. Just the thought of some of her Johns make her sick to her stomach. Rosie's friend Tasha just IM'd her and asked her to hit the track with her tonight. Rosie is torn, she doesn't want to go but in the past Tasha has always gone out with Rosie even if she didn't want to, plus Rosie doesn't want her friend out there alone.

____

____

____

Homework: Think about the different trauma bonds that you may have similar to Rosie and share in your individual therapy.

____

____

____

____

____

Week 4
Rediscovering Your Past

Introduction: What was your earliest happy memory of your childhood? Please share it now with the group.

____

____

____

How does memory work? The way that we look at the past is often affected by how we experience life right now. It is like looking at our past through a filter, only seeing those things that match our current experiences. If we are struggling now, we remember those things that are similar in our pasts and negate or don't recall the good memories. In the same manner it is common to only look at the good in the past in regard to our current relationships.

Why do I have blank spots in my memory? Memory may be seen as laid down in layers, like that of an onion that has been cut down the middle. If you have gone through trauma in your past, your memories may be laid down in these layers that block the remembering of the memories in the next layer. As you face the memories in the first layer, that layer dissolves and the next layer of memories come to you.

Why do my newly remembered past come with such strong emotion? Traumas that we experience when we are young are often too drastic to handle. Our young minds lay down the layers to handle the trauma and to continue to live our lives. The memories and strong emotions are both trapped within these layers until later released. Because you did not deal with the trauma or emotions before, when released, these memories often come with the original emotions. It is important to work through these emotions and trauma in your individual therapy.

It seems that all my memories are either totally bad or totally good, why does this happen? This is once again your mind filtering out the memories based on your present experiences. You are struggling with family; thus all memories of family are bad. You are having a good moment with your pimp or "street family" and so those memories are all good. It is important to look at all our memories, both good and bad. This allows us to have more of a foundation in reality to both understand our past and to move on into the future.

Can I just go to the core of my memories and get my therapy done quickly? The danger of going through all your memories too quickly is that you won't be able to handle the strong emotions coming at you all at once. Your mind made the layers to help you to survive. It is wise to go through each layer, one at a time with a therapist that you have grown to trust.

There is a blessing in this memory work! The layers of memories have trapped both good and bad memories of your past. Working through the layers will release some good memories of the past. Good memories that will help you find your purpose in life and having a real picture of your past allows you to stand on a firmer foundation!

Please consider the following scenarios and how you would advise Rosie:

Rosie doesn't have any memories before age six when she lived with her Mother and Father. At age six her parents divorced, and she went to live with her Mother. Should she try to remember those early memories, why or why not?

____

____

____

and/or. . .

Rosie believes that her parents are totally bad, there is nothing good about them or her time with them between her run-a-ways.

____

____

____

and/or. . .

Rosie is so angry at her Mom as the Mom doesn't remember ever leaving Rosie alone with her father or other male family members, so how could they have molested Rosie?

____

____

____

and/or. . .

Rosie lives with her Mom but believes that her Dad is great as he allows her to do what she wants when she visits him. Mom says that her Dad was very abusive when she was young, but Rosie doesn't remember any of that and thinks that her Mom is just being bitter.

____

____

____

and/or. . .

Rosie is in a shelter and is on probation for trafficking. She only has good memories of being on the street and misses the freedom and the drugs that she was able to enjoy.

____

____

____

and/or. . .

Rosie is beginning to remember very painful memories of molestation or abuse in her childhood. She wants to stop therapy and be "numb" once again.

____

____

____

and/or. . .

Rosie is angry as many people in her life want her to remember how "bad" her trafficker was. She remembers the love, the glitter, and that he "loved her."

____

____

____

Homework: Please share in your individual therapy the memories that this group exercise has begun to trigger. Try to share both good and bad memories of past and present relationships. Viewing the past accurately is critical in viewing the present and future through a filter without distortion.

____

____

____

____

____

____

____

____

____

____

Week 5
Dealing with Your Anger

What is the worst thing you have done in a fit of anger?

____

____

____

____

What is anger?

Anger is an emotion or feeling. How we use anger determines the outcome and the consequences made by our behaviors. If not controlled, anger may drive your behavior and responses to the situation resulting in regrettable actions. Anger is an emotion and is internal. Aggression is a behavior and is external. It is possible to be angry and not be aggressive.

Please answer the following questions:
Is anger bad?

____

____

____

____

How can anger be useful?

____

____

____

____

How have you controlled your anger?

____

____

____

____

When we can take control of our levels of anger/tension, it's likely we can better respond to difficult situations and make better decisions. You can determine which technique works best for you. Not one technique will work for every situation; use your discretion.

Understand what makes you angry- The first step in breaking a habit is knowing that you have a habit. Try keeping a journal of when, how and what makes you angry. You will start to learn what triggers your anger and you will then gain some control over the anger.

Put yourself in the "shoes" of another person - This is called empathy, trying to understand why a person is doing the things that he or she is doing that tend to get you angry.

Listen to your thoughts - When you get angry, "catch" your thoughts--what is your thinking when angry? This will help you to better understand yourself and the reasons for your anger. You can then decide if you want to allow these thoughts to trigger your anger.

Take a walk/walk away/time-out from the situation - Gives you time to process what has happened and think about your actions and how to respond next. Is it worth the argument? What's at stake? Walking away from an intense situation for 10 minutes can save a relationship, save a job, and save you from guilt or regret later on.

Learn how to laugh - When we are angry, we are very serious people; learn how to laugh at yourself! Don't laugh at others as this will usually just make them more angry!

Muscle relaxation and breathing - Relaxing your muscles can alleviate the tensions you may feel in your shoulders and back, your abdomen, and your arms and neck. In a brief moment, your body will start to relax which will allow you to re-evaluate the situation in a more calming state. One of the most common relaxation methods people uses is the deep breathing technique. Deep breathing will allow your heart rate and tension to lower.

Learn how to be assertive - It is important to get your needs met without being a doormat or aggressive to others.

Talk about your anger - Beginning to communicate about your anger will allow you to not just yell or stuff your anger inside.

Become a problem solver - Pain in your body means something is wrong you have physically hurt yourself in some way. Anger indicates that something is wrong emotionally. Try looking at anger as a problem to solve, not just react to.

Learn to forgive - This is the best way to control anger and will be the subject of two other group sessions.

These 10 techniques for controlling your anger will be explored more in your individual therapy.

How would you advise or encourage Rosie in the following scenarios?

Rosie is so angry at her parents for not being there for her in her childhood, they were either gone working or disappearing into their relationships and/or drugs. . .

____

____

____

and/or. . .

Rosie is angry at her probation officer for telling her what to do and how to do it. She wants the freedom to do what she wants on the streets. . .

____
____
____

and/or. . .

Rosie is angry at her boyfriend as all he cares about is drugs and sex, but he doesn't seem able or willing to take care of her. . .

____
____
____

and/or. . .

Rosie's pimp seems to always be angry at her; she gets beaten for things she does and doesn't do. . .

____
____
____

and/or. . .

Rosie's sisters in the stable or family seem always to be angry with her, even though she tries so hard to do her quota and to fit in. . .

____
____
____

and/or. . .

Rosie is so angry at men and women that are her "customers." She is disgusted by them but has to act as if she is excited to be with them. . .

____
____
____

and/or. . .

Rosie is so angry at herself that she punishes herself with cutting and other abuses to her body. . .

____

____

____

Homework: Please share in your individual therapy the memories that this group exercise has begun to trigger.   It is important to work out ways that you can deal with your anger, addressing issues in the past, present and for better control of your anger into the future.

____

____

____

____

____

____

____

____

____

____

____

____

____

____

____

____

____

____

____

Week 6
Freedom from the Past – Forgiveness

Why is it easy to forgive our children for something they did wrong, but we are often quick to reject a boyfriend/girlfriend, husband/wife?

____

____

____

What is forgiveness? Is it a sign of strength or weakness?

____

____

____

How do you forgive? Why is it important to forgive?

____

____

____

Remember that Forgiveness and Trust are two different things. Forgiveness can happen one moment in time, but trust has to be earned!

Forgiveness is a process. For one person it may be easy to forgive, another person may need more time.

Steps for Forgiveness: "I forgive you!"

1. Express what has hurt you.
2. Confront the person/situation that hurt you, unless it puts you in further danger.
3. Share what you need to forgive or close the doors on the past.
4. Express your willingness to forgive.
5. Maintain your forgiveness, don't hold on to the pain.

Steps for Forgiveness: "I am sorry!"

1. Be humble and express the importance of the relationship.
2. Allow the person to express their pain.
3. Allow the person to share what they need in order to forgive.
4. Express verbally that you are sorry for what you have said or done and ask for forgiveness.
5. Don't repeat the behavior.

How would you help Rosie in the following scenarios?

Rosie was abandoned by her father when she was young. Her father now wants a relationship with her, but she hates him. . .

____

____

____

and/or. . .

Rosie was sexually abused as a child by a family member and her Mom has told her to just let it go, move on with her life. . .

____

____

____

and/or. . .

Rosie loves her Mom, but the Mom keeps choosing her current boyfriend/lover over her. . .

____

____

____

and/or. . .

Rosie's best friend brought her to a party and was raped by her friend's pimp boyfriend. He had her rape filmed and threatened to put the film on social media if she didn't do what he wanted. . .

____

____

____

and/or. . .

Rosie's sister in "The Game" keeps telling her "daddy" what she does, just to get her into

trouble. . .

____

____

____

and/or. . .

Rosie is angry at the world, but especially at her parents, her probation officer and those in authority. Why can't they just accept what she says, why can't they trust her?. . .

____

____

____

and/or. . .

Rosie is so angry at men, for what they have done to her in the past. She hates servicing them in "The Game". She can never see herself with a boyfriend or husband or any normal romantic relationship. . .

____

____

____

and/or. . .

Rosie can forgive everyone around her, but she can't forgive herself for living on the streets, for all that she has done

____

____

____

Homework: Please share in your individual therapy the memories that this group exercise has begun to trigger. It is important to look at areas in your life that are holding you "trapped" in the past. Work with your therapist on how to forgive others or to ask for forgiveness for those that are important in your life.

____

____

____

____

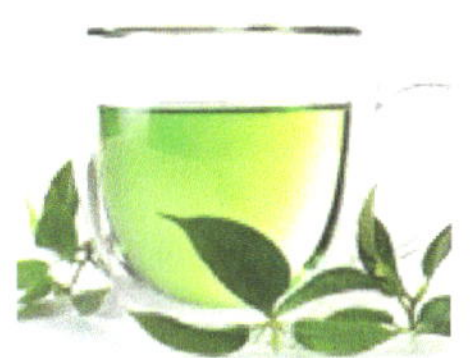

Week 7

Learning how to chill (Symptom Management)

KEEP
CALM
AND
RELAX !!

When you were in "The Game", what did you do to relax?

____

____

____

What you do now to relax or be at peace?

____

____

____

It seems those that have been in trauma have a very hard time relaxing. What causes this continued stress or tension?

____

____

____

Combat soldiers often talk about an inability to relax. They are afraid that if they let down their guard that they will be attacked and killed. Veterans in wars like Viet Nam talk of taking drugs to stay awake and then to be able to sleep. This practice often led to addictions that carried over into civilian life when they returned to America.

This sense of danger all around you is often seen on the "streets" or in "The Game." The same misuse of drugs may be needed to get through "tricks" and at some point to just "crash and rest."

Learning how to relax is an important technique to learn to break the cycle of addictive behavior on the streets. Learning how to relax in a safe environment is critical in this new learned behavior.

Let's practice a technique called "progressive relaxation." Our muscles are designed to either tighten or relax. When a muscle gets stuck in the middle it is called a "cramp" or "charley-horse." If we can teach you to relax in normal clothes here and now, then you can learn how to relax anywhere.

One of the Group Therapists will now guide you through the following muscle groups: Fist, Fists, Arms, Shoulders, Eyebrows, Eyes, Lips, Mouth, Neck, Back, Thighs, Feet and Abdomen.

The Therapist will first encourage you to tighten the muscle group, hold that tightness and then let go. As you notice the difference between tight and relaxed musles, you can be more aware of where you feel tension in your body and learn to relax that part of your body.

The Therapist will also encourage you to take slow, deep breaths through your nose and breath out through your mouth and say the word "relax" to yourself. You will notice that you will begin to relax with each breath released.

Now that you are relaxed, please consider the following scenarios of Rosie and how you would advise her. . .

Rosie has to take drugs before stripping or turning "tricks" and has to keep selling herself in order to have monies to pay for the drugs.

____

____

____

and/or. . .

Rosie can't sleep without drugs to "knock her out" or to "feel no pain." Now, out of "The Game", how can she afford these drugs?

____

____

____

and/or. . .

Rosie can't relax as just when she is ready to sleep or being at peace, she startles awake or has a flashback of the past.

____

____

____

and/or. . .

Rosie can't stand to be touched. When she is touched she feels like she will jump to the ceiling or collapse on the floor. Sometimes she just wants to strike out at the person touching her.

____

____

____

and/or. . .

Rosie has a hard time not thinking sexual thoughts when people stop to talk with her; she believes that they have a sexual motive or want something from her.

____

____

____

and/or. . .

Rosie is always wired, with or without drugs. She is able to relax with marijuana but refuses any prescription medications. She has not had good experiences with people using drugs and medications to control her

____

____

____

Homework: Please share in your individual therapy the memories that this group exercise has begun to trigger.   Practice the progressive relaxation and other healthy techniques to better relax.

____

____

____

____

____

____

____

Week 8

Addiction – Sex, Drugs, and Food

An addiction is when one has to have more and more of something to get the same high or even feel normal. An addiction is also when you have withdrawal symptoms when you no longer have what you are addicted to.

What addictions do you have in your life?

____

____

____

What have you tried to do to break out of the addiction?

____

____

____

What worked and what did not work to break the addiction?

____

____

____

Addictions common to "The Game" include sex, drugs and food. The first step in breaking an addiction is understanding the addiction cycle. We talked of an addiction cycle last session in a person taking drugs to stay awake and then to fall asleep as well.

A person may have to take drugs to "strip" or walk the "track." Soon the person takes more and more drugs to overcome the disgust of having to be on display or to do things sexually that he or she did not want to do. Sadly, then the drugs are needed to just feel normal.

To break out of an addictive cycle involves making a choice to stop. You really cannot replace an addiction; it must be a conscious and dedicated choice. This often involves an accountability partner, a therapist, an outpatient program and in many cases an inpatient treatment program.

Your healing from these addictions may involve learning healthy sexuality, eating and how to deal with stress and life without drugs.

Please consider the following scenarios in helping Rosie:

Rosie must take ecstasy before she can strip, it seems that she has to take more and more ecstasy each time she dances.

____

____

____

and/or...

Rosie binges on sweets whenever she gets a chance, it makes her think that she can eat whatever she wants, whenever she wants to.

____

____

____

and/or...

Rosie has to have rough sex with her boyfriend, or the sex doesn't seem to be real or she cannot feel anything.

____

____

____

and/or...

Rosie has to have sex quite often, separate from "turning tricks." Boyfriends outside of "The Game" always involve frequent sex.

____

____

____

and/or ...

Rosie can't just take one drug or drink; she must take or drink so much that she blacks out or loses time.

____

____

____

and/or. . .

Rosie doesn't strip and is not part of "The Game" anymore. She still has to use drugs to "face" the world.

Homework: Please share in your individual therapy the memories that this group exercise has begun to trigger.   Please share with your therapist the different areas that you believe you still have an addiction. This can be the beginning of your "choice" to break your addiction cycle.

Week 9
Real Charm – Finding Friends & Social Skills

Think about the best friend you had in the past. How would you describe that friend?

____

____

____

What are the inside characteristics that you want in a friend?

____

____

____

What outside characteristics do you want in a friend?

____

____

____

How do you get new, good friends?

____

____

____

It is said that the best way to get friends is to be a friend; how does that work?

____

____

____

Some people like to have many shallow friends and others have just a few close friends; which type of person are you?

____

____

____

The danger of being in "The Game" is that you have learned how to "turn on" the charm, but not how to go deeper into a friendship. We learn that in order to have a deeper friendship it is important to share about yourself and allow the other person to also share about him/herself. As we are more open in communication, the other person feels safer to also share more.

Friendships are often developed quickly in intense, often traumatic situations. These friendships, though, often break apart when the intense situation is over. Deeper, longer lasting friendships develop over time.

Consider what your interests or hobbies are. You may want to develop friendships around your common interests and enjoy doing something together. Perhaps to attend a church, go back to school, join a club as ways to meet people that are away from "The Game."

Consider how you would help Rosie in the following scenarios:

Rosie just came out of "The Game" and has no "square friends." She feels very loney and wants to contact some of her old pals on the streets.

____
____
____

and/or. . .

Rosie is told that her fellow sister-in-laws (wife-in-laws) are her friends, that she can trust them. She is hurt often when they "rat/squeal" on her.

____
____
____

and/or. . .

Rosie believes that if she spends time on the streets with her old friends that they will respect her and not push her to go back to drugs or "the life."

____
____
____

and/or. . .

Rosie doesn't know who she can trust with sharing her heart. She has been hurt so many times and people have used what she shares to hurt her more.

____

____

____

and/or. . .

Rosie feels that she can only have male friends as they don't compete with her. She doesn't understand how the girl friends seem to always stab her in the back.

____

____

____

and/or. . .

Rosie believes that men only want to have sex with her, that they can't be a real friend.

____

____

____

and/or. . .

Rosie doesn't know how to have more "healthy" friends.

____

____

____

and/or. . .

Rosie doesn't know how to take off the mask and be real, not to pretend that everything is okay and that she is always smiling.

____

____

____

Homework: Please share in your individual therapy the memories that this group exercise has begun to trigger.   Please share with your therapist the struggles that you have with friends and your desire to have real friends that you can also be "real" with.

Week 10

Love and Relationships

How would you describe the perfect boyfriend/girlfriend?

____

____

____

How would you describe the perfect husband/wife? Would these characteristics be the same as for the perfect boyfriend/girlfriend?

____

____

____

How would you describe "Love?"

____

____

____

How would you describe "Trust" and how does it relate to "Love?"

____

____

____

There are at least three types of love, involving sexual, brotherly and a sacrificing love. A sexual love can be intense, but only fulfilling for a short time. This sense of physical touch to ecstasy may be sought after to the point of being an addiction, similar to a drug high and then relaxation.

Brotherly or sisterly love is a close friendship that cannot be broken and is a love that "watches each other's backs." A sacrificial love is one that you are willing to give totally of yourself to another person, even to the point that you give up what you want to make the other person happy.

To have a lasting relationship is to have all three loves combined. The friendship love becomes so deep and long lasting that the sacrificial and sexual love is a natural outgrowth of the first love. When both persons have the three loves combined for each other, the relationship deepens further.

There is only one true test of a "true love" that you can trust the other person. Trust is a virtue that says you can rely on or know that the person will be there when you need him/her. This test is simply time together. A dating relationship over the course of a year allows you to have your first argument and to see how you come through the argument. The long dating period will show you if the other person is consistent in their love, then you can trust or rely on them.

Another issue to watch for is a "flip" characteristic. A coin has two sides, heads and tails, both sides are needed to make it a coin. We are attracted to certain characteristics in another person but need to know that there may be a flip side to this attractive characteristic. Consider the following and fill in the blank for the "flip" characteristic:

"He wants to take care of me." Flip characteristic <u>"He wants to control me!"</u>

"He loves to have fun." Flip characteristic <u>"He is lazy!"</u>

"He/She is so handsome/beautiful." Flip characteristic ________________________

"He is so spiritual." Flip characteristic ____

"He handles money so well." Flip characteristic __________________________________

"He is so intelligent." Flip characteristic ____

The only thing that helps you to know if your loved one has the "flip" characteristic is time; over time he or she will reveal their true self.

Please consider the following scenarios and how you would advise Rosie:

Rosie begins to date in her "square" world, but every date ends with sex and then the boyfriend seems to lose interest in her.

____

____

____

and/or. . .

Rosie wants to have a steady boyfriend and eventually a husband. She judges each potential boyfriend on how he is in bed. This is most important to her.

____

____

____

and/or. . .

Rosie has a steady boyfriend, he is good in bed, but he doesn't provide any money; in fact he allows Rosie to "dance" to make money for both of them.

____

____

____

and/or. . .

Rosie has a good friend who is always there for her and never has hurt her, but she can't date him. It would be too weird.

____

____

____

and/or. . .

Rosie has a boyfriend who wants to take care of her, he even times how long it should take for her to go to the store and back to him. He always wants to know where she is.

____

____

____

and/or. . .

Rosie has just met a military boyfriend and he rotates to another duty station in less than three months. He wants her to come with him and maybe even get married.

____

____

____

and/or…

Rosie has been with her pimp for quite some time; now he wants to marry her.

and/or…

Rosie has three boyfriends, "Tom" is good in bed, but doesn't support her financially at all. "Richard" is young, closer to her age, a good provider, but somewhat immature. "Harry" is almost twice her age, a very good provider and could teach her much about life. How does she make a choice?

and/or. . .

Rosie wants to meet a healthier boyfriend and eventually husband. Where does she go to meet such a man?

Homework: Please share in your individual therapy the memories that this group exercise has begun to trigger. Please share with your therapist the struggles that you have with relationships and the characteristics that you are seeking in a partner.

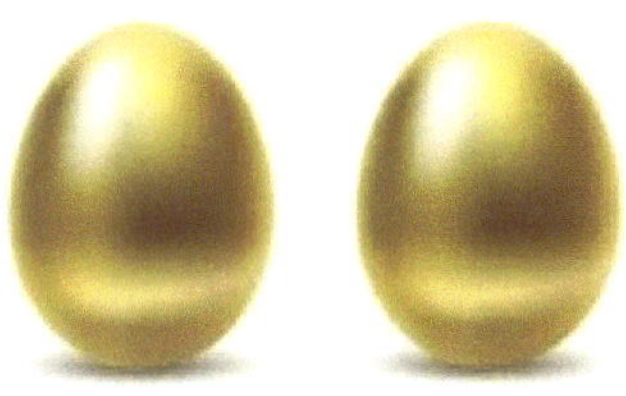

Week 11
Dealing with Money in a Square World

What does the following saying mean: "She has champagne tastes on a water budget"

____

____

____

It is difficult to earn $250 or more for each "trick" and typically $1000 per night and then go to a "square" job, the square job often paying minimum wage.

Typically, the amount of money that we make equals the amount of money that we spend. Prostitution, stripping and other forms of "The Game" can turn over large sums of money each day. Given that much of the money is kept by pimps or handlers, you still see large sums of money.

Given the fact that most, if not all of your money is taken by your handlers, you really did not have that much money in "The Game"-- money to buy things other than what the pimp wanted you to spend. If you hid money, you ran the risk of being "beat down."

It is important to change how you look at working and how you look at making money. As you transition into the square world you will make less money each hour, but your expenses should also go way down, i.e. no expensive clothes or drugs.

You also may need to look at social welfare services or aid until you can get on your feet financially. Be careful of people trying to give you a quick way of making money as they may just be trying to take advantage of you once again.

As you ponder going into the square world financially, let's look at Rosie and how you might advise her. . .

Rosie is having a hard time making ends meet with her square job; she is thinking about turning a trick to just get some quick money, just one more time. . .

____

____

____

and/or. . .

Rosie still has contact with her wives-in-law and they are offering her a loan of money. Should she? It can't hurt.

____

____

____

and/or. . .

Rosie has a need to use weed to relax, but she has no choice but to use the monies that she could use for food to buy it.

____

____

____

and/or. . .

Rosie feels shame in applying for food stamps or any type of social aid, but she needs food. . .

____

____

____

and/or. . .

Rosie dreams of having money in "The Game" and sometimes wishes that she could just turn a few tricks again.

____

____

____

and/or. . .

Rosie doesn't know what she can do now in working; her pimp said that she was only good being a "bitch."

____

____

____

and/or. . .

Rosie thinks that she can now keep all the money if she goes back into "The Game."

____

____

____

Homework: Please share in your individual therapy the memories that this group exercise has begun to trigger. Please share with your therapist the struggles that you have with relationships and the characteristics that you are seeking for in a partner.

____

____

____

____

____

____

____

____

____

____

____

____

____

____

____

____

Week 12

Dreams – Artistic Expressions & Future Planning

If I had no restrictions, the thing that I would most like to create is. . .

____
____
____

What will you want to have accomplished at the end of your life?

____
____
____

Given these lifetime goals, what would you like to accomplish in five years?

____
____
____

Given these five-year goals, what can you do for five minutes each day towards these goals?

____
____
____

When one has gone through trauma, especially prolonged and intense trauma, life becomes one of survival. It is easy to be serious all the time and to not feel that one can laugh or have joy.

The healing that you have begun to have is important to continue the rest of your life. This involves at least two areas, recapturing your childhood and being creative in your life.

To recapture your childhood is to be able to once again enjoy what you did before you experienced all the trauma in your life. This may be watching cartoons, movies and TV shows that bring laughter into your life once again. It may be coloring in a coloring book, or even playing with toys with or without other children present. You may get into board games or card games, start to go hiking once again, camping--the options are as limitless as your imagination.

Being creative is being able to make something that reflects your heart and soul. This could be painting, baking, cooking, building something, sewing. Again the options are limitless as your imagination.

Today you will be given the opportunity of doing some artwork to start these creative juices flowing again in your life. One option is painting a "Circle of Life" with watercolors or acrylic paints.

The inner circle is that which you see yourself now and the outer circle is what you want to happen in the future, your creative self. After painting the circles, spend some time in sharing your artwork.

It is also a good time to interact what you have gained from the group and how we can make it even better for future participants.

Homework: Please share in your individual therapy the memories that this group exercise has begun to trigger. Please share with your therapist the struggles that you have with how you view yourself now and how you want to see the creative, fun self in the future.

www.ingramcontent.com/pod-product-compliance
Lightning Source LLC
Chambersburg PA
CBHW040049240726
48664CB00004B/1118